JOHANN SEBASTIAN BACH

Italian Concerto, Chromatic Fantasia and Fugue

and Other Works for Keyboard

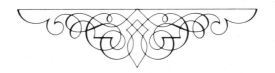

From the Bach-Gesellschaft Edition

DOVER PUBLICATIONS, INC., NEW YORK

Published in Canada by General Publishing Company, Ltd., 30 Lesmill Road, Don Mills, Toronto, Ontario.
Published in the United Kingdom by Constable and Company, Ltd.

This Dover edition, first published in 1987, is a new selection of works from two volumes of the set *Johann Sebastian Bach's Werke*, originally published by the Bach-Gesellschaft in Leipzig. The *Italian Concerto* and the *Overture in the French Style* (together comprising Part II of the *Clavier-Übung*) are from Volume (Year) 3 (1853; first volume of the series *Clavierwerke*; edited by C.F. Becket). The remaining works are from Volume (Year) 36 (slated for 1886, actually published 1890; fourth volume of the series *Clavierwerke*; edited by E. Naumann).

Manufactured in the United States of America
Dover Publications, Inc., 31 East 2nd Street, Mineola, N.Y. 11501

Library of Congress Cataloging-in-Publication Data

Bach, Johann Sebastian, 1685–1750.
  [Harpsichord music. Selections]
  Italian concerto, Chromatic fantasia and fugue and other works for keyboard.
  Reprint. Originally published: Leipzig : Bach-Gesellschaft, 1853 (Johann Sebastian Bach's Werke ; v. 3) (BWV 971, 831).
  Reprint. Originally published: Leipzig : Bach-Gesellschaft, 1890 (Johann Sebastian Bach's Werke ; v. 36) (other works).
  Contents: Italian concerto : BWV 971—Overture in the French style : partita in B minor : BWV 831—Chromatic fantasia and fugue : in D minor BWV 903—[etc.]
  1. Harpsichord music.   I. Title.
M22.B11D63   1987   86-755110
ISBN 0-486-25387-2

Contents

After the items that comprise Part II of the *Clavier-Übung*, the pieces appear in the order of their BWV (*Bach-Werke-Verzeichnis*) numbers. Titles and places and times of composition given here are based on the 1980 *Grove*.

Richard Jones, author of the catalogue of J. S. Bach's works in the 1980 *Grove*, considers BWV 917, 918, 919, 922, 947 and 948 to be of doubtful authenticity.

Italian Concerto, BWV 971

4   *Italian Concerto (BWV 971)*

Andante.

Italian Concerto (BWV 971)　7

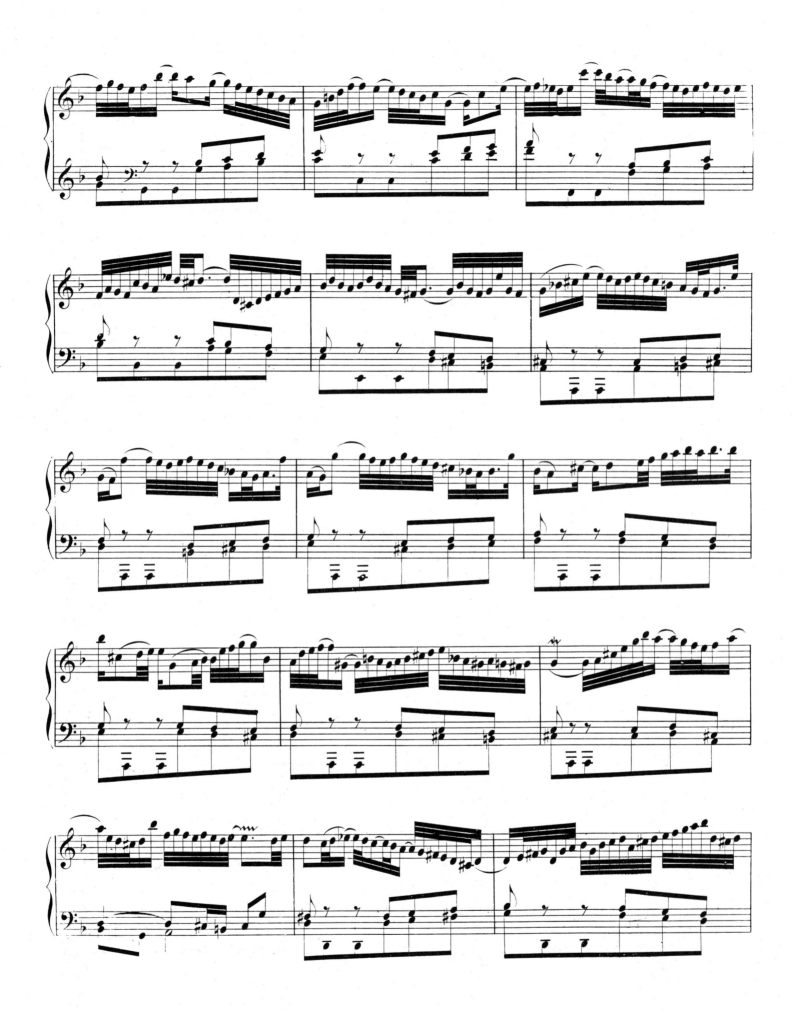

10 *Italian Concerto (BWV 971)*

14   *Italian Concerto (BWV 971)*

Overture in the French Style [Partita] *in B Minor,* BWV 831

Ouverture.

18   *Overture in the French Style (BWV 831)*

Courante.

Gavotte I.

Gavotte II.

Passepied I.

Passepied II.

Passepied I Da Capo.

Sarabande.

Bourrée I.

Bourrée II.

piano

Gique.

30   *Overture in the French Style (BWV 831)*

Prelude and Fugue in A Minor, *BWV 894*

Praeludium.

36   *Prelude and Fugue in A Minor (BWV 894)*

Fuga.

Prelude and Fughetta in F Major, *BWV 901*

Praeludium.

Fughetta.

Prelude and Fughetta in G Major, *BWV 902*

Praeludium.

Prelude and Fughetta in G Major (BWV 902)   49

Fughetta.

Alternative Prelude, BWV 902a

Praeludium.

Chromatic Fantasia and Fugue in D Minor, BWV 903

Fantasia.

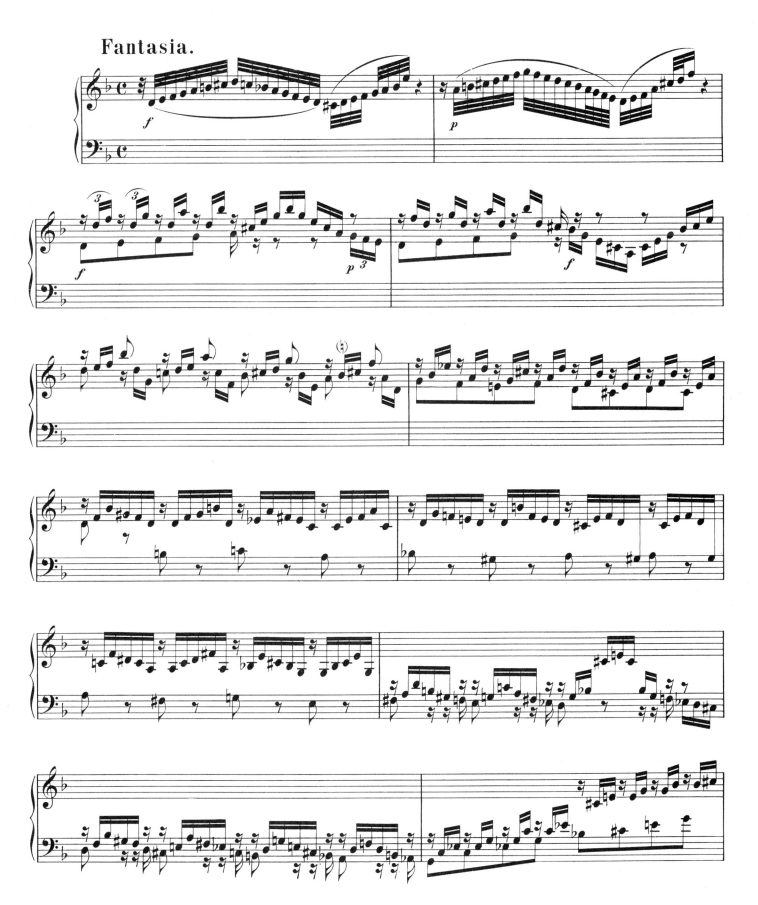

Fuga.

Variant of the Opening, *BWV 903a*

From this point on. the music is substantially the same as in the main version.

Fantasia and Fugue in A Minor, BWV 904

Fantasia.

66   *Fantasia and Fugue in A Minor (BWV 904)*

Fuga.

Fantasia and Fugue in A Minor (BWV 904)

Fantasia and Fugue in C Minor, *BWV 906*

Fantasia.

Fuga.

(incomplete)

Fantasia in G Minor, BWV 917

78   *Fantasia in G Minor (BWV 917)*

Fantasia on a Rondo in C Minor, BWV 918

80 *Fantasia on a Rondo in C Minor (BWV 918)*

Fantasia on a Rondo in C Minor (BWV 918)

Fantasia in C Minor, BWV 919

84   *Fantasia in C Minor (BWV 919)*

Prelude {Fantasia} in A Minor, BWV 922

86 *Prelude in A Minor (BWV 922)*

Fugue in C Major, BWV 946

Fugue in A Minor, BWV 947

94 *Fugue in A Minor (BWV 947)*

Fugue in D Minor, BWV 948

96 *Fugue in D Minor (BWV 948)*

Fugue in D Minor (BWV 948) 97

Longer ending.

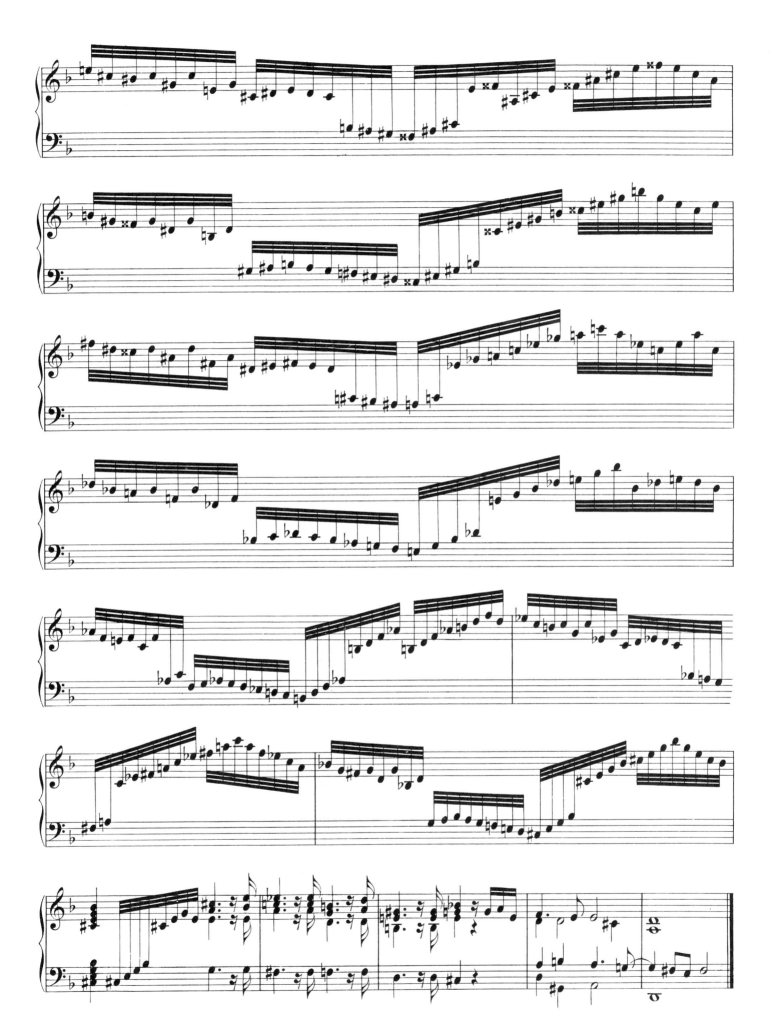

Fugue in A Major on a Theme of Albinoni, *BWV 950*

Fugue in A Major on a Theme of Albinoni (BWV 950)